GRIDIRON

Tony Benyon & Kevin Macey

FONTANA/Collins

First published in 1987 by
Willow Books
William Collins Sons & Co. Ltd
8 Grafton Street, London W1X 3LA
First issued in Fontana Paperbacks 1988

Design and Editorial by Bookbourne Limited
the Old Farmhouse, Newton, Sleaford, Lincs NG34 0DT

Printed and bound in Great Britain by
William Collins Sons & Co. Ltd, Glasgow

CONTENTS

INTRODUCTION

"This game is all about everyone trying to beat the crap out of everyone else" —
Jim McMahon, the Chicago Bears quarterback.

6

Introduction

Why, with all the options open to sportsmen, should anyone want to play Gridiron? The answer is simply that American Football is the only sporting activity a fully grown man can involve himself in, apart from ballet, where he can be seen in public wearing tights and Dynasty style shoulder pads. Of course there is also the odd guy who is drawn to the game by a deep rooted need to smack the heads off other guys.

What is a Knuckle Ball? What is a Linebacker doing when he is Stunting? And should it be allowed in Public? All these questions, and many you haven't even thought of asking, are answered within these pages.

This book is published for the football fan who either desires a rudimentary knowledge of the games rules or a deeper insight into the people who play it. So, smear grease marks onto your face, pop in your gumshield, pad up your sensitive parts, and if you are under the age of thirteen make sure you read this book in the presence of an adult.

CHAPTER 1

THE GAME

SCORING POINTS

American Football involves two teams going to war against each other. (It also involves drugs, sex, rock 'n' roll, Fort Knox and a clutch of politicians who played before sufficiently protective helmets were introduced – see later chapters). Should players on either side still be alive after playing for sixty minutes, instead of a draw being declared the points scored by each team are added up and the one with the greater number of points is declared the winner. When this happens to a team regularly throughout the season the head coach gets to keep his job.

To understand how points are scored we must first of all examine the field of play known as the 'Gridiron'. At both

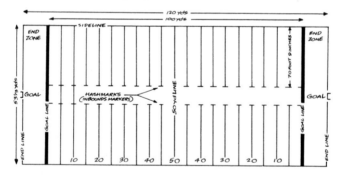

ends of the Gridiron are areas called 'End zones'. In medieval times they were called 'Cemeteries' and came into being because they were the most convenient sites for burying the mortally wounded when a game was in progress.

Scoring Points

The teams set out to place the ball into their opponents'end zone, an act known as a 'Touchdown', worth a total of six points.

Two points are scored when a quarterback is caught in possession of the ball in his own end zone.

A conversion goal is kicked after a touchdown and is worth one point, and a field goal scores three points. The latter is attempted when the offense have failed to gain yardage due to their game plan being useless. When this happens regularly throughout the season the head coach doesn't get to keep his job.

11

LINE OF SCRIMMAGE

The team with the ball, The Offense, is given four opportunities, 'Downs', to move it ten yards up the pitch towards the end zone belonging to the team without the ball, The Defense .
The offense starts each move by lining up across the width of the pitch facing the defense. This formation is known as the 'Line of Scrimmage'.

The line of scrimmage

All the action from the scrimmage takes place around the quarterback. He's the player who appears to be doing something rather unsavoury to his colleague in front of him.

12

SNAPPING

The player in front of the quarterback (the centre) passes the ball between his legs (snaps) straight to the quarterback who either passes or throws it to an available team member, while everyone else on the pitch attempts to spread everyone else over the ground, apart from the officials who are there to make sure they are spread over the ground legally.

YARDAGE AND PUNTING

The offense are allotted four downs to gain ten yards: if they fail to gain them, they forfeit the ball to their opponents. At each scrimmage the quarterback releases the ball to a player who becomes the 'Ball carrier'. He in turn is savaged by the defense and the distance from the scrimmage to his blood stains, marking the spot where he was grounded, is measured by the 'Chain Gang'.

The Chain Gang

If the offense fail to gain ten yards and they are too far away to kick a field goal, they kick or 'Punt' the ball as far and as high as possible downfield. The opposing team allocate a player 'Receiver' to catch the ball and to carry it back into the other half of the Gridiron. The point where he is pressed into the ground as the opposition attempt to build a human pyramid on top of him, becomes his team's scrimmage line.

SCORING A TOUCHDOWN

If the offense continues to gain yardage, and finally a ball carrier crosses the goal line, a touch down is scored. To celebrate, the player dances profanely for several seconds and then cuddles, slaps, gropes and french kisses (not an easy act while wearing a face guard) as many of his team mates as he can (lingering over those of whom he is particularly fond) and if the game is being televised he rushes to a camera on the sidelines, pulls off his helmet (often over-eagerly removing his head) and mouths 'Hello Mom' while pointing a single finger towards heaven. One can never be sure if this is to signify that his mom has recently passed away or if God is actually a woman after all.

KICKING A CONVERSION

After a touchdown the kicker is brought on to attempt a
conversion which takes place directly in front of the
goalposts. The defense try to block the kick by forming
another human pyramid (See P. W. Krvnicks 'Gridiron and
the ancient Egyptians'). A conversion should not be missed.
If a Japanese kicker misses too often he has to fall on his
sword, if an American pro misses too often he gets kicked off
the team and has to fall back on his savings.

The Game

CHAPTER 2

EQUIPMENT

PADDING

Below is a diagram showing how the essential parts of the American footballer's body are protected from full frontal assaults by Sherman tanks and nuclear ground-to-player missiles.

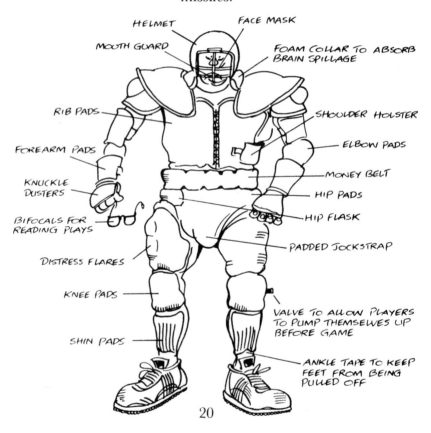

HELMET

FACE MASK

MOUTH GUARD

FOAM COLLAR TO ABSORB BRAIN SPILLAGE

RIB PADS

SHOULDER HOLSTER

FOREARM PADS

ELBOW PADS

KNUCKLE DUSTERS

MONEY BELT

HIP PADS

BIFOCALS FOR READING PLAYS

HIP FLASK

PADDED JOCKSTRAP

DISTRESS FLARES

KNEE PADS

VALVE TO ALLOW PLAYERS TO PUMP THEMSELVES UP BEFORE GAME

SHIN PADS

ANKLE TAPE TO KEEP FEET FROM BEING PULLED OFF

20

EXTRA PADDING

Footballers wishing for a more attractively-developed body
may use some of the extra padding available for a more
musclebound shape.

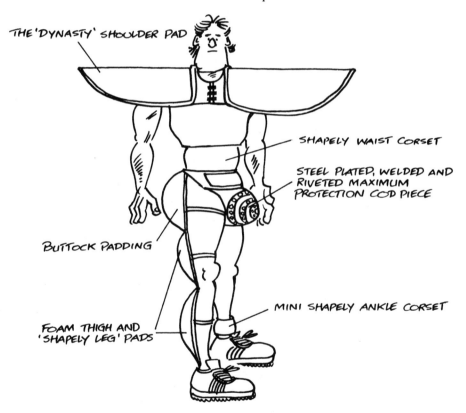

THE 'DYNASTY' SHOULDER PAD

SHAPELY WAIST CORSET

STEEL PLATED, WELDED AND
RIVETED MAXIMUM
PROTECTION COD PIECE

BUTTOCK PADDING

MINI SHAPELY ANKLE CORSET

FOAM THIGH AND
'SHAPELY LEG' PADS

21

UNIFORMS

A player's shirt and pads need to be flexible and durable.
Flexibility is needed so players can actually get them over
their padding and durability is essential because they are so
bloody expensive.

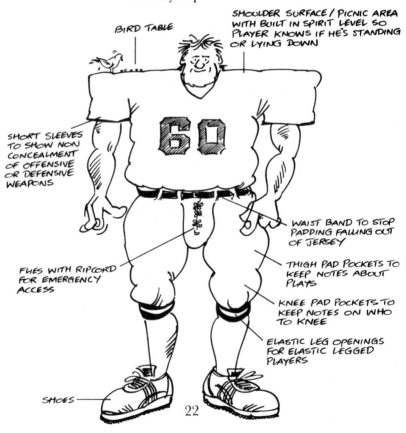

BIRD TABLE

SHOULDER SURFACE / PICNIC AREA
WITH BUILT IN SPIRIT LEVEL SO
PLAYER KNOWS IF HE'S STANDING
OR LYING DOWN

SHORT SLEEVES
TO SHOW NON
CONCEALMENT
OF OFFENSIVE
OR DEFENSIVE
WEAPONS

WAIST BAND TO STOP
PADDING FALLING OUT
OF JERSEY

FLIES WITH RIPCORD
FOR EMERGENCY
ACCESS

THIGH PAD POCKETS TO
KEEP NOTES ABOUT
PLAYS

KNEE PAD POCKETS TO
KEEP NOTES ON WHO
TO KNEE

ELASTIC LEG OPENINGS
FOR ELASTIC LEGGED
PLAYERS

SHOES

22

Equipment

HELMET AND FACE GUARD

Helmets are supposed to protect players, but in many cases they harm players during a head-first hit. Softer, padded helmets are due to be brought in which protect the wearer but also do as little damage as possible to the victim. This won't necessarily spoil the game.

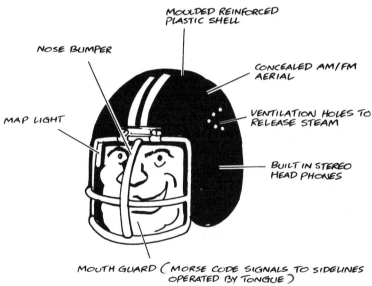

MOULDED REINFORCED PLASTIC SHELL

NOSE BUMPER

CONCEALED AM/FM AERIAL

MAP LIGHT

VENTILATION HOLES TO RELEASE STEAM

BUILT IN STEREO HEAD PHONES

MOUTH GUARD (MORSE CODE SIGNALS TO SIDELINES OPERATED BY TONGUE)

CHAPTER 3

THE PLAYERS

THE SOFTIE

At the age of six the Softie was as mentally advanced as he is at twenty six. He was also six feet tall and weighed one hundred and forty pounds. He rose above his contemporaries like a colossus and they endowed him with a god-like status. The reason for their adoration was that in spite of his physical supremacy he never once bullied them, and was quite content to let them use him as a battering ram to break down the doors of closed drug stores. When any one of his friends were threatened by street gangs they would run to hide in his immense shadow, from where they hurled abuse at their would-be assailants, who failed to realise the Softie would burst into tears if he so much as trod on an ant.

The only person to remain unimpressed by his gentleness was his father, who considered him to be utterly wet and likely to grow up to be a pansy. He introduced him to the manly art of boxing, but the boy couldn't understand why he should hurt anyone or why anyone should want to hurt themselves by hitting him.

At sixteen he was shunted into a football team. He was six feet eleven and a half, and weighed two hundred and eighty pounds. He was useless in defense but brilliant at centre, protecting the quarterback from those who wanted to damage him. His father was delighted to see him acclaimed as a man's man in a man's world. He never lived to see him move in with the quarterback after they exchanged rings.

The Softie

THE HUSTLER

The hustler has a tongue as slippery as a soaped eel. No-one can talk himself out of a tight corner so ably, but then most people wouldn't have got themselves into the corner in the first place.

With his mouth jammed on fast forward he will attempt to sell you anything he can lay his hands on, which often includes items you already own. More drastically he can talk you into a 'deal' meaning that a 'money-making opportunity' will lose you all your worldly possessions and also the future earnings of your as yet unborn great grandchildren.

Why isn't this man a zillionaire playing real monopoly with the other fat cats in the financial funfairs of the world?

Because one or two ounces of his grey brain jelly were left back in the depot when the stork delivered him. He makes money but then it seems to vanish, he knows not where.

The hustler's amoral wheeling and dealing is not confined to the locker room or to his team mates, it also extends to the field of play and the opposition. The only means of resisting his banter is to shut your eyes and jam your fingers into your ears while humming loudly to yourself. He keeps his place in the team because when the opposition shut their eyes and jam their fingers into their ears they become rather vulnerable to well-designed offensive plays.

THE SUPER STUD

The Super Stud started to play football because it was the only way he knew of showing his shapely thighs and groin off to as many women as possible in public without being arrested. Standing on the sidelines in his tights, his heavy lidded eyes seek out female targets and give them a hot lingering look that says 'This is what you're missing sweet thang, I mean can you live without it?'

A natural extrovert, he chooses to play as a wide receiver so that after scoring a touchdown he can demonstrate how supple his body is with a celebratory rhythmic dance of triumph, while at the same time flicking a cutie in the crowd his telephone number scrawled on a retouched photograph of himself pumping iron.

The concept of remaining celibate the night prior to a match is anathema to him. Whichever town he finds himself in, and whatever the security, he will have a female companion for the night if it means winching her up from the street or her hang-gliding onto his balcony. This man's image of himself would be severely dented if he were to be seen without a brace of beauties pasted to his gyrating body.

The Super Stud lives in a home designed as a chamber of mirror-tiled seduction. Even an eye level grill transforms at the flick of a switch into a water bed.

The Super Stud

The Players

FRANKIE'S MONSTER

The cities of the world are filled with insane scientists striving to achieve world domination by various dastardly means. There are also insane coaches who spend their later years searching for that certain something with the potential of making the greatest football players ever. They hang around college games, high school games and cheap bars, always on the look out.

One night, when he least expects it, a coach trips over something in a dark alleyway. Clutching his bruised toes with one hand, he lights a match with the other and falls backward from shock. Two wide-open bloodshot eyes return his stare. Turning to run away, he witnesses the floor of the alleyway rise upwards. It's just a drunken waster standing up – all eight feet of him.

Cackling with delight, the crazed coach trains his prodigy in a deserted gymnasium, where he develops the monster's body and attempts to do the same with his mind. The day comes when the coach gets him a trial. He plays brilliantly. Defensive players bounce off his gigantic form. He is signed immediately. Match day approaches, and the monster divides his silent time between practising with the team and the dank cellar where he lives with his demented mentor. He stands open-eyed in a dark corner throughout the night. When match day comes he scores ten touchdowns before the

32

Frankies Monster

old coach clutches his chest and drops dead. Unblinking, the monster walks off into the night, never to be seen again.

THE BODY POPPER

The body popper doesn't have arms like Popeye or the physical presence of a grizzly bear standing on its hind legs, what he does have is a contortionist's control of his body. From birth he has been gifted with the ability to dislocate and relocate his limbs at will, and to spin on his head or bore holes in the ground with his rapidly rotating buttocks. Away from the dance floor he virtually ceases to exist until he's on the gridiron and the ball has been thrown to him, then he becomes a blur of action with just a hint of aftershave. "What's happenin'?" is the most complicated combination of words he ever utters and because of his failure to communicate verbally no one knows if he's married or even has a home. He is further alienated by a permanent pair of headphones playing the sounds he thrives on, and by his mirrored shades.

During the game he can slip through a fist of defensive players like liquid, by dismantling his body and reassembling it on the other side of them. Once in the end zone his celebratory movements melt the plastic turf and cause seasoned disco dancers to weep from envy. Nicknamed 'Liquorice', because he goes through any defense at speed, he also goes through his playing career with equal speed. He is doomed to burn himself out and to click off just as easily as he clicked on. When he retires he will assume an even lower profile than the invisible man and never be heard of again unless he has a party, then he'll be heard coast to coast.

The Body Popper

THE ROCK STAR

The rock star is incapable of singing or of playing the guitar. He turned to football as his only chance of ever getting applause. He also hoped the game would attract large numbers of groupies and artificial stimulants as well as vaults filled with bullion.

He runs on to the field of play with a padded jockstrap, flexed and oiled biceps and long hair flowing from beneath his helmet, striking more poses in five minutes than an average heavy metal guitarist strikes in five months.

After scoring a touchdown he pretends to rev up an imaginary Harley Davidson and then plays an equally invisible guitar before imitating a mincing Freddy Mercury.

In conversation he refers to the team as 'the band' and attempts to convince the manager that they should cut a single and record a promo video, just like all the major teams. While he waits for stardom he practises a wild head-banging life style by smashing up motorway cafe toilets, by treating women in a disgustingly sexist manner and by working out who he will have in his entourage.

Lying in a bed draped with pale strangers he dreams about throwing colour televisions from hotel windows while making sure the light remains on; not only so he can continue looking at himself in the mirror for as long as possible, but also because he's afraid of the dark.

The Rock Star

THE RELIGIOUS FREAK

The religious freak was converted in mid air when he was on target to sack a quarterback. By the time his helmet had unsprung several of his opponents' ribs he was convinced the resulting damage was the will of God (even though there is no theological evidence to suggest that God has any interest in gridiron). He immediately crossed himself as he backed away stamping on his victim's throat.

He now leads a prayer meeting in the locker room before each game and asks for the Almighty's strength to pulp the opposition.

He is very much an Old Testament man, approving of muscular Christianity and an eye for an eye, and a cracked tibia for a cracked tibia. He is totally unable to turn the other cheek. If the Romans had ever thrown him to the lions you can be sure he would have taken several of the lions with him. His local church members appreciate his conversion. Their door-to-door charity collection has never had such healthy results even now that he's stopped turning people upside down and shaking out their pockets.

Instead of showering after the game and washing down his iron hard body he goes immediately to the confessional where he washes his hands of his heinous acts.

The Religious Freak

THE DAY RELEASE PRISONER FROM DEATHROW

People who commit crimes are normally shunned by decent society unless they happen to be sports stars. The public will accept a linebacker who has an amphetamine problem, but not a President. A mass murderer can be an acceptable TV chat show guest if he becomes a heavyweight boxer. The large amounts of money these people make for their backers, promoters, syndicates, television stations and organised crime does go a tiny way towards helping.

Football can transcend penal sentences, and along with reborn Christianity and bribes the day release prisoner from deathrow can soon dovetail back into the pro game. It is difficult to outstare a man who you know has dynamited a pizza bar when his order for a 'deep-pan mushroom with extra anchovies' took more than twenty minutes. His small, cold, unblinking eyes depict a dark and dangerous world that it is best not to know too much about.

A proven mass murderer who plays in the defensive line can be a great addition to the team. Any offense would think twice about blocking him without his permission. If his presence alone doesn't threaten the opposing players, the two prison guards flanking him with pump-action shotguns probably will.

40

The Day Release Prisoner From Deathrow

The Players

THE
TERMINATOR

On seeing the terminator transform an averagely competitive
football game into footage from 'Driller Killer' it is hard to
realise he has a first class degree in business studies.
Strikingly handsome, with a showbiz smile, he appears to be
a composite Yuppie cruising effortlessly to his first million,
aided by 'insider information'.
His home is a designer-converted warehouse filled with
expensive possessions which still, rather showily, retain their
price tags.
The terminator's gory on-field activities are far removed
from his off-field lifestyle. His playing style has been
cultivated for maximum return. He regards football as his
easiest means of raising capital to move into commodities.
Obeying the first law of supply and demand he is giving the
public what they want, a brutal, heartless war machine that
any self respecting girl could take home to mummy.
Not only is he highly paid for playing, but his Robert Redford
looks have heaped endorsements upon him. He also guests on
television chat shows in heavy rotation. A witty and
articulate King Kong is always deeply mined by the media.
His ambition is to leave football before he's thirty and to

42

become a multinational, but the ferocious and dangerous way he plays the game may result in brain damage, in which case he intends going into politics, with a strong chance of making it to the top.

THE MASOCHIST

The masochist is driven to seek mental and physical pain by a dark urge deep in his subconscious. The former he acquires from his marriage to a shrew-like woman with a tongue capable of opening sealed envelopes. The latter he partly achieves by demolishing unsafe buildings with his head but mostly by playing gridiron. A masochist's ideal world is populated by sadists, and there are more sadists per group of ten in football than in any other sport apart from dentistry. In a late night bar a friend will advise the masochist not to have a twenty-third beer but to go home before his wife gives him hell; he stays for another six beers then asks the barmaid to put some lipstick on his collar before he leaves. He is also the only player in the universe who relishes a confrontation with the 'Day release prisoner from deathrow' and will taunt him with shouts such as, 'Hey, skunk breath! While you've been inside I hear your wife's been unfaithful to you only once – with the Red Army!'
One reason the masochist craves pain is his feeling of guilt about the lifestyle he lives. He wants to be punished for tucking into a three-steak breakfast while people all over the world are going hungry. He could give up football, go on a diet and dedicate his life to relieve international famine, but the pay is rotten so he rises from the breakfast table and goes to shave, and with any luck to cut himself.

THE COLLEGE BOY

The College Boy is well-mannered, straight-backed, fresh-faced and has the kind of marine haircut you can scrub your nails with. Everyone he meets he calls 'Sir', from his old college principal to a drunken bum sprawled out in the gutter. He comes from a small, dull town where he married the small, dull girl from next door and has two small, squeaky-clean but dull children. Adultery, as far as he's concerned, is something that only happens in television soap operas and the Bible.

When he isn't helping old ladies across the road or performing other charitable work, he plays football. Walking onto the field of play he's Mr Niceguy. The sun reflects off his halo and dances over the polished enamel of his perfect teeth as he passes by the cheerleaders and quietly prays for their salvation. From the moment the game starts, the sun slips behind a dark cloud and he becomes a demented loudmouth. Steeped in the 'Up team' mentality he is determined to see his side do well, even at the cost of his own life, or preferably someone else's.

Once the game is over, his clean cut image switches itself back on. He passes the stretchered casualties he helped to damage and deals out a prayer book to each one. Back in his fireside rocking chair he plays his favourite hymns and John Denver songs on guitar.

The College Boy

CHAPTER 4

ON THE SIDELINE

THE HEAD COACH

A head coach must be overweight, with either a short bullish neck or no neck at all. He (few women become coaches) should have a range of two facial expressions, burning anger and ecstatic relief. For the rest of the time he should remain utterly deadpan. His main skill is psychologically dominating 280lb head-bangers spaced out on Colombian talcum powder. When one of these brain-damaged mutants demands he shut his mouth or risk having his internal organs externalised, the coach must be able to reduce the offender to a mound of quivering, apologetic jelly by raising a single masterful eyebrow, or be pulped. In the sidelines he walks the same precarious line as a lion tamer, cracking a whip and making his awesome charges pose incongruously on medicine balls and paw the air and snarl, instead of eating him whole as they could so easily do.

The coach's other job is to overview the game plan, exploiting his own team's strengths and pinpointing the weaknesses of the other. These are technical means for protecting his own quarterback while instructing his defense on how to knock the daylight out of the opposition's quarterback.

He also has the complicated task of walking up and down the sidelines while holding a clipboard and shouting simultaneously. Not many ex-players are capable of this complicated combination, as head blows take a terrible toll; for further proof try listening to the television commentators.

SPECIAL TEAM COACHES

Special teams all have their own coaches responsible to the head coach. The cheerleaders' coach is often a woman, who has to rehearse her charges to perfection. Their morals are also her responsibility. It is bad news when a cheerleader turns to drink or decides to have carnal knowledge of as many men as possible, especially during a game. A drunken, leering cheerleader mooning at male spectators is not a pleasant sight.

The players have an offense and a defense coach. The offense coaches are often sacked for being too offensive, and the defensive coaches are usually known as lawyers. Their main responsibility is bailing players out of jail and bribing the officers or witnesses concerned. The morality coach gives advice on sex and drugs, providing updates on prices and availability. The coach coach is in charge of transport.

Most coaches are ex-players, which explains why women are not coaches. Ironically, during their playing days they were only averagely successful, which must mean they didn't listen closely enough to themselves, or if they did they didn't take their own advice.

Any of the above coaches may one day become head coach if he makes the proper moves, like cutting the brake cable on the right car or finding a source for the rare Amazonian poison that is untraceable in coffee.

Special Team Coaches

SPECIAL TEAMS AND RESERVES

More people stand on the sidelines of a gridiron game than pay to see some British soccer games. Why do the special teams and reserves stand so close to the sidelines? Simply so that when an opposing ball carrier is pushed, tackled or runs over the sidelines into them, it provides the whole crew with an opportunity to sit on his head, snap a few ribs and dislocate a variety of limbs under the pretext of helping him back onto the pitch.

The greater the number of players on the sidelines also means the better the camouflage for concealing the plays being called to the quarterback. It is true to say that the sidelines were introduced by television to offer viewers even greater drama – coaches slashing their wrists, players hugging, kissing, crying, or beating up a loudmouth in the crowd. The players' union wanted cameras on the sidelines so players coming off the pitch can tear off their helmets and mouth 'Hello mom.' It saves the expense of having to phone home so often.

The special teams consist of players with special interests. Some like drinking, some frequent discos, while others prefer flesh-orientated activities. Players who enjoy a combination of all three activities do their training separately in intensive care wards.

THE CHEERLEADERS

Cheerleaders are young girls with slim attractive figures. They are selected on their looks and not so much on their intellectual ability. They must have the piano keyboard smiles of the retards in toothpaste commercials, with wide unblinking eyes and certifiable fixed grins. The latter expression must remain constant throughout blizzards, monsoons and while being run over by a burning truck. Each girl's figure must be trim and firm; it shouldn't judder or bounce about uncontrollably during excessive physical activitity. The girls should also not have criminal records or wear glasses, slings or braces, and because large parts of their flesh are on view to the public they should not be too heavily tattooed.

The brainwork demanded of a cheerleader is not excessive, but a basic memory and a facility to spell are important. For example, being able to spell the name of the team she is cheering for is of critical importance. Nothing could be more embarrassing than facing a large crowd of fans and shouting 'Give me an, er, er, sorry, er . . .' The last golden rule for cheerleaders is that when wearing a short ra ra skirt it is an absolute necessity to remember to check that one's knickers are on.

Cheerleaders

58

CHAPTER 5

PLAYER POSITIONS

ASSIGNMENTS

A team is made up of 45 players approximately distributed
among the following categories:
Kicker 1
Punter 1
Tight Ends 2
Quarterbacks 3
Wide Receivers 4
Running Backs 5
Defensive Linesmen 7
Linebackers 7
Defensive Backs 7
Offensive Linesmen 8

Each of these players has a number on his uniform as follows:
Punters, Kickers, Quarterbacks (Offense) 1-19
Running Backs (Offense), Corner Backs, Safeties 20-49
Center (Offense), Linebackers (Defense) 50-59
Interior Linesmen (Offense), Defensive Linesmen 60-79
Wide Receivers, Tight Ends, Split Ends, Flankers 80-89
Defensive Linesmen (In addition to 60-79) 90-99

The players are numbered so that officials may spot an
interior offensive linesman if he illegally receives a forward
pass, and also for the police to identify whoever is responsible
for illegally killing either another player or an official. Alas,
during a game not many television commentators are the
victims of homicidal acts.

THE WIDE RECEIVER

The wide receiver has to be capable of incredibly flexible movement. Throwing dummies on the run while jumping and catching a ball in mid air takes a combination of athleticism, timing and intuition with just a dash of insanity. No wonder he is tagged with nicknames like 'Crazy Legs', 'The Rubber Phantom' or 'The Crazy Rubber Legged Phantom' or even 'Derek'.

It is more than essential that a wide receiver should lose his marker or markers and make himself a clear target for the quarterback. To do this he pretends to run one way and then runs another (a dummy). Sometimes he may fool the inexperienced defender (a complete dummy) but a more experienced player will stay as close to him as a second skin. To avoid him, the receiver has to dig into all his resources of skill and experience (he has to foul him without an official seeing).

The most difficult decision facing a wide receiver is what choreographed dance movement he should perform after scoring a touchdown. Finding a new stylish way of gyrating the pelvic area is no easy task for someone who hasn't trained on Broadway. The post-touchdown ritual is equivalent to the immediately recognisable signature with which an artist completes a painting.

Wide Receiver

Player Positions

THE RUNNING BACK

A running back is so called because he takes the ball from the quarterback and runs with it towards the opposition's end zone. This is more difficult than it first sounds, because between him and his destination is the opposing defense. He has two options, first to run around them and secondly to run between them. If the latter is his ordained route, his own big men will try to carve a gap for him to run through. Should they fail, an assortment of large fellows will jump on his head or any other available part of his anatomy, leading to countless fractures, breaks and crushed internal organs.

If a short distance needs to be gained for a first down it is usually the running back who is requested to gain it. He takes the ball and then head-first he sets off for yardage. The defense responds with the classic movement where two defensive linesmen block him and set him up for a third to make a brutal hit on him. Often the sharp sound of colliding helmets will echo around like pistol fire. Rarely is it pistol fire; players are not supposed to be armed, but then they're not supposed to play dirty either.

After each run the back may retire to the sidelines where he can receive oxygen, a variety of injections, legal advice, surgery or psychiatric care. At the end of each week he receives a pay cheque which, if he's lucky, will exceed his medical bill.

THE KICKER

Kickers are usually the team eccentrics. They are not oddballs because of the continual hammering their brains have taken from hits, they are weird before they even start to play. One needs look no further than the guys who kick in the NFL. As well as the fruitcakes who kick in their bare feet, there are also Englishmen. In most other ball games players are smart enough to know how to tie their own shoe laces and to stay out of the midday sun. Not so in gridiron.

Kickers are the ultimate funny-farm candidates. Loners, they thrive on pressure rather than avoid it. There may be no experience like winning the superbowl by kicking a field goal in the dying seconds of the game, but equally there must be no feeling like missing a field goal in the dying seconds and losing the game. Only a complete drongo would ever want to take such a responsibility, but there are no shortage of guys around without a full deck so there is never a shortage of kickers.

Poundage is not important to these players but two legs are a minimum requisite (there are few one legged kickers any more). The kicker sometimes takes the punts too. An ideal punt goes so high that it comes down with icicles on. The icicles make it more difficult for the receiver to catch and often skewer him to the ground; this is known as a good punt.

THE QUARTERBACK

The quarterback is the most influential player on the pitch. He calls the shots, passes the ball, does the interviews and pulls the chicks. He also spends the greatest time in intensive care.

It is essential for a quarterback to have 'an arm' which means that he actually has two but one in particular is a gift from God. An exceptional arm can launch a ball for seventy yards with pin point accuracy through an eye of a needle or preferably flat and powerfully through the body of a defender.

Quarterbacks must be able to 'bootleg' which means taping albums onto cassettes and selling them to his team mates. It also means short yardage 'rushing' when his receivers aren't available. Should he be under considerable pressure with no one to pass to or sell cassettes to he must 'scramble',which is a forwards movement where the gaining of yardage is superseded by self preservation.

The quarterback is the nerve centre of the team which is why the opposition set out to hurt him as much as they can. 'Sacking' is when he is savagely maimed in possession of the ball, an 'accidental injury' is the term used for him being wiped out after he has released the ball. Not many modern quarterbacks live to gain such nicknames as 'The Old Fox' or 'Grey Beard'.

Quarterback

THE TIGHT END

The tight end is not so called because he has a drink problem or a disinclination to part with money, nor is it a reference to an uncomfortable physical abnormality. The name comes from him being tight on either the left hand or right hand end of the five interior men in the offensive line at the scrimmage. The last man to make up the minimum of seven players in the offensive line is the split end.

The tight end is the most versatile player in the game. He is capable of blocking like a center, receiving a pass or carrying the ball through a cacophony of colliding helmets, animal grunts and fragmenting bones. He has to be more mobile than an interior linesman, weigh between 230 and 240 pounds, stand well over six feet, have safe hands and crazy legs.

He's worth watching if you are a spectator and if you are a defender you really have to watch him. He can outpace linebackers and bemuse a corner back who is suddenly confronted by him and a wide receiver.

Silent and proud, he doesn't mind more glamorous players getting all the praise while he does all the work. He's quite happy to return home in the evening and pursue his hobby of making lifelike dolls and then playing with them using a dozen small steel needles.

Tight End

THE INTERIOR LINE

Centers, Tackles and Guards

The center is the 20 stone player who snaps the ball back between his legs to the quarterback and then blocks the nose tackle or any other defensive player the fates decide to hurl at him. It is essential that he should have good hearing and be free of flatulence. A sudden discharge of noxious gas at a critical moment could distract the quarterback's attention with disastrous results.

The two guards and the two tackles help the center to either create a safe pocket for the quarterback to throw out of, or attempt to crash into the defensive line to conjure a gap for a running back to skip through.

Traditionally, the center and tackles are the biggest men in the team, capable of dishing out punishment as well as being in receipt of it. They are naturally aggressive with a lurid range of insults capable of upsetting even the most steely-hearted defender, and they favour questions such as 'Didn't I see your mother out with . . . last night?' or 'Hey man, your wife's better in bed than I thought,' or else they use quite unprintable insults like 'Xxxx xxxxxx xxxxxxxxx xx?' or even 'Xxxxxxx xxxxxxx xxxxxxxx xx xxxxxxxx xxxx xxxx!' They make defensive players so mad that they put

themselves offside as they rush over to kill them, or worse still they actually do kill them which in some circumstances can lead to a sending off.

THE DEFENSIVE LINE

The Nose Tackle, Ends and Linebackers

The defensive line is made up of one defensive tackle and two ends. The former is also known as a nose tackle, a name unrelated to his facial appearance or to the part of an offensive players person that he has a preference to tackle. He is a pumped-up 260-270 pounds of barely-suppressed mayhem, with a purpose in life to break up the offensive play by either wasting the ball carrier or by integrating the quarterback with the fabric of the pitch. Ideally, a nose tackle should have a low centre of gravity to drive hard and low into an opponent's body.

The defensive ends are lighter and more agile than the tackle, but their intention is also to process the ball carrier into a non-vegetarian spread or to 'heat-seek' their way to the quarterback. Behind them are the linebackers, a pack of ravenous hunters more lethal than the Mafia hit men they have the power to terrify.

The defensive team like to have an identity separate to the rest of the team and often select their own nicknames. Hence the New York 'Sack Exchange', or the Giants 'Crunch

Bunch' and the Dallas 'Doomsday Defense'. If you have your own team then get yourselves a nickname, but remember you have to live up to it. You can call yourselves the Aldwych Armageddons, but if the eleven of you don't add up to 500 pounds other teams will give you new nicknames like the 'Nerds', the 'Wimps' or 'Those about to die'.

THE DEFENSIVE BACKS

The Safeties and Corner Backs

Two corner backs and two safeties make up the last line of defense. The former mark the wide receivers. They are fast and agile and either appear utterly brilliant or incredibly dumb. When a wide receiver swerves brilliantly, leaps to catch a 60 yard pass with one hand, performs another devastating swerve and then sprints with smoking soles into the end zone to score a touchdown, without a doubt the corner back comes out looking like a quintessential nerd. Where was he?

In the future, no doubt some hot-shot wizard of the surgical implant will be able to fix up a corner back with a second set of eyeballs in the back of his head, so that he can watch the ball without taking his eyes off the receiver.

Should a corner back make an interception, and carry the ball for a dozen precious yards, his ecstasy is likely to burst his jock strap. There can be no greater delight apart from intercepting and then running to score a touchdown. When this happens, he must immediately be thrust into a straightjacket and tied down with weights or else he'll complete several laps of the world.

Defence Backs

A safety marks whichever players are acting defensive ends. They are unsung heroes, often bitter and twisted. If a quarterback finds a photograph of himself abused by biro he should look no further than the safety. However, he shouldn't look down dark alleyways late at night, unarmed.

CHAPTER 6

STRATEGY AND FORMATION

STRATEGY

Strategy is co-ordinated by the head coach. It is designed to exploit the strengths of his team and to protect its weaknesses. Instructions are sent to the team from the coach on the sideline, or onto the field of play with a replacement player, or by sly hand signals, but rarely by the cheerleaders using their pom-poms to transmit semaphore.

Players have to know the team play book by heart, because when they go into a huddle with the quarterback, they must come out of it knowing exactly where they should be and what they should be doing. Meanwhile, the defense will be arranging themselves in a formation to counteract the formation they think the offense will take up. Gridiron is really a microcosm of life; it's based on deception and kicking a man when he's down.

The strategic side of gridiron is often compared to chess. In truth, there is no similarity; chess players do not wear helmets or even the smallest amount of padding, perhaps a cushion to sit on is all the equipment they have. A grand master would be of little use to the Chicago Bears, apart from being a mid-game snackette.

Before the game, a plan will have also been formulated to restrict the opposing team's star player. This means hitting him as early as possible and as hard as possible. If the plan fails, they have to resort to off-field tactics like planting dope in his clothes at half time and making an anonymous call to the drugs squad.

Strategy

OFFENSIVE FORMATIONS

'Offensive formations' only used to refer to lines of youths mooning in the streets after the pubs closed, until gridiron erupted on our television screens. Now we know it to mean the variety of positions taken by the offense at the line of scrimmage, and the planned combinations of movements executed after the snap. To follow these formations use the key below:

Q	Quarterback	FB	Fullback
RB	Running back	TB	Tail back
SE	Split end	HB	Half back
FIB	Flankerback	WB	Wing back
TE	Tight end	C	Center
T	Tackle	G	Guard

It is immediately noticeable what a cunning game gridiron is. For example who are the tail back, the split end and the wing back, the flankerback, the full back and the half back? Well, the full back, the half back and the tail back are other names for a running back. The flankerback and the split end are other names for wide receivers. There is a very definite logic behind the names; just remember they are defined by the positions the players adopt when they line up at the scrimmage, taking into account the alignment of Mars and Uranus in the first quarter of . . . . .

82

Offensive Formations

PLAYS

After the offense adopts its preselected formation, the ball is snapped and to the uninitiated the players proceed to run about like headless chickens. It is almost impossible to learn about plays from watching the television, because when the action is reshown in slow motion the transmission is always interrupted by someone in an advanced state of hysteria, while an unseen hand vandalises the picture by scribbling all over it.

A 'passing play' depends on the designated receiver freeing himself from his marker and making himself available for the pass, while his team mates attempt to make the defense believe they are the target.

A running play depends on the offensive line manufacturing a hole in the defensive line large enough for the ball carrier to leap through. It is no good hoping a hole will appear by natural causes as players become incapacitated through old age or sickness, it must occur immediately by explosive brute force or better still without the use of explosives.

The following diagrams show how formations develop into play combining brawn and brains, uppers and downers, anabolic steroids and medicated foot powder, and all the other elements essential to all modern sports apart from synchronised swimming.

Plays

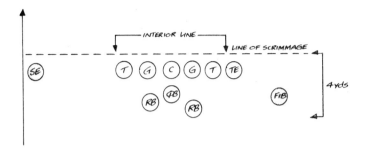

Above is a diagram of the Pro-Set Formation. Note what
follows in the diagram below.

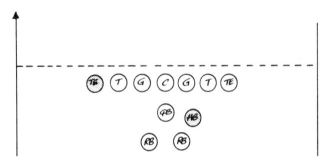

The split end has split and the flankerback has vanished,
while another tight end has sneaked on to replace him. The
offensive line hide a half back and two running backs, hoping
the defense can't see them. The defense is so stunned by this
cunning ploy that after the snap they fall back almost a yard
in astonishment, which is why it's called the Short Yard
Formation.

THE STREAKER FORMATION

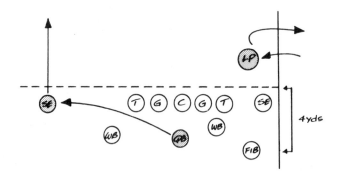

In the Streaker Formation the offense have two split ends on the line and no running backs or tight end. They also have a twelfth 'player' who positions herself in the opposition's territory: she is a streaker or Large Pods.

The moment before the snap, the center says to his opposing nose tackle, 'Oh wow! A streaker! I've never seen pods like them!' or, 'Good grief! Is that your wife over there stark naked?' The nose tackle will find it impossible not to look around as will the safeties and the cornerbacks. When the snap takes place, the defense see a clutch of wide receivers apparently running towards the streaker. Not to miss out, they all move over to get a better look. The streaker dives back into the crowd, while the quarterback passes to his left side split end who strolls over to touch down.

The Streaker Formation

THE RABID DOG FORMATION

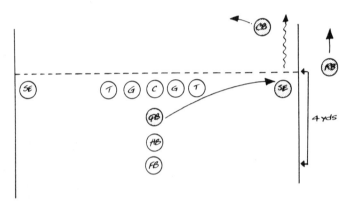

The Rabid Dog Formation is similar to the Streaker but relies more on using fear as opposed to voyeurism. Prior to the snap, the right side split end raises his voice loudly and in horror when a dog appears on the sidelines with a frothing mouth (soap suds). 'Rabies! Oh my God! Rabies!' he exclaims. The defense stares in horror at the dog as it starts to run along the sideline towards their end zone. Only when it reaches the zone do they realise the split end has been following it carrying the ball after receiving a sly pass from the quarterback. This play, 'like the Streaker', should only be used once during a game as should the 'I Don't Believe It, Man, The Cheerleaders Forgot To Put On Their Knickers' Formation.

The Rabid Dog Formation

THE COMPLETELY LOONY FORMATION

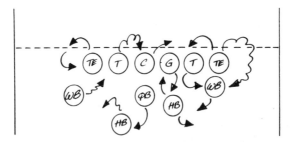

In the Completely Loony Formation the offense line up as closely to each other as possible when they need to gain a few inches for a first down.

The ball is snapped to the quarterback and the entire offense start to run away from the defense while screaming gibberish and rolling their eyes to suggest an outbreak of mass insanity. The defensive players are further confused as their opponents blow them kisses and promise them a good time in the showers after the game.

The defense is even more dumbfounded. They have no planned response for apparent insanity and as they look to the sideline for help the quarterback removes the ball from beneath his shirt and hops into the end zone, making sure beforehand that it is his opponent's end zone. This formation and play should only be used once in a career.

The Completely Loony Formation

DEFENSIVE FORMATIONS

Defensive work is based on making moves that anticipate the moves the offense will make. For example, as the offense line up in the streaker formation a good defense will nod at each other knowingly. 'The old streaker formation', they whisper between curled lips, and then they continue with a gleam in their eyes, 'The fools! Don't they realise we're all gay?'

The offense are, of course, in full knowledge of their opponents' sexual preferences which is why the streaker they have chosen is male. The defense react with further sniggering. They know the offense thinks they're gay, but in reality they've switched to an all-heterosexual lineup. But wait! The streaker isn't a man at all! Once onto the field of play, the fake appendage comes off and reveals a woman.

What the offense was not supposed to know the defense knows, the offense know they know, but do they know the defence know they know or don't know they thought they knew? The offense of course know they knew they know they knew they know they knew, and both teams base their plays on that knowledge with the hope their opponents don't know.

A brilliant defense will have predetermined that a really brilliant offense will cover both possibilities with an hermaphrodite streaker, but do either team realize the streaker has rabies? In all honesty we won't know until the snap.

The Defensive Formation

THE RED INDIAN FORMATION

Unlike the offense, the defense can move around as they wish, making adjustments to their formation right up to the snap. A cornerback can stand shoulder-to-shoulder with a defensive end and then pull back at the last second, or slide along the line of scrimmage to stand facing a split end.

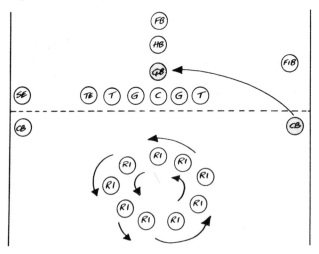

The Red Indian Formation above consists of two backs positioned wide on the line of scrimmage while the remaining defensive players run about in a circle chanting in loud voices. The quarterback, who has never seen anything like

this before (hopefully), looks to his coach for advice once he's in possession of the ball. Should he pass, hand off or bootleg? While he turns to the sidelines and the offensive line look on in paralysed bemusement, the right side cornerback runs in on his blind side and splatters him across the field, a loss of ten.

DEFENSIVE PLOYS

The defense must disconcert the quarterback whenever possible. Anything that distracts his attention away to the sidelines is a positive move. The drugs squad making a raid on the bench, a ritual beheading or King Kong eating a section of the crowd are all old favourites. It is difficult for a quarterback to say to himself,'Wow! Isn't that King Kong eating the part of the stadium where my folks are? I'll check it out after I've made this fifty yard pass to the split end out there on the sideline where those naked Japanese girls are being beheaded and just to the left of where it looks like the head coach is being machine gunned . . . what the!!!'
A double take is all that's needed to allow the defense to blitz and beat the quarterback into the ground like a tent peg. The more orthodox defensive formations are the traditional nickle-and-dime and penny defenses, evidence that gridiron began in a country obsessed by materialism. Obviously these formations were so named before rampant inflation and should now be known as the 10,000 dollar and 100,000 dollar formations, the latter being the upgraded sum a center and his guards will accept before allowing the defensive ends to slide between them and shred the quarterback (this is known as taking a bribe or more commonly as professionalism).

KICK OFF FORMATIONS

The game starts with a kick off after the toss has been won or lost. The winning team normally choose to receive the kick so they can start a drive with a four down series. The kicker hoofs the ball high enough to get snow on it and far enough to need a passport. A kick receiver tries not to be hammered into the ground as he catches it and then runs as far into the opposition's territory as he can. The other team quite naturally hit him as hard and as fast as they can, making it impossible to get him off the ground without a rake, in the hope that he will fumble the ball.

The worst kick receivers are polite players who stop and say 'Thank you' before they get splattered, and ex-motorcycle messengers who won't accept responsibility for the ball unless someone on the other team signs for it.

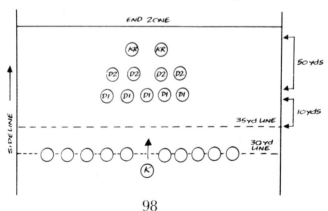

98

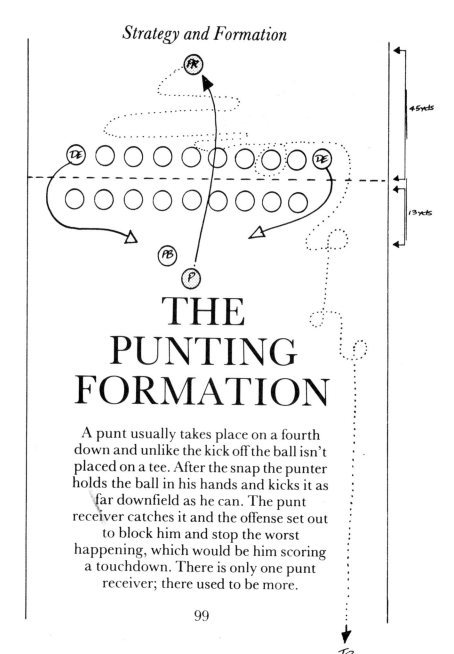

45yds

13yds

THE PUNTING FORMATION

A punt usually takes place on a fourth down and unlike the kick off the ball isn't placed on a tee. After the snap the punter holds the ball in his hands and kicks it as far downfield as he can. The punt receiver catches it and the offense set out to block him and stop the worst happening, which would be him scoring a touchdown. There is only one punt receiver; there used to be more.

99

TO END ZONE

FIELD GOAL AND CONVERSION FORMATION

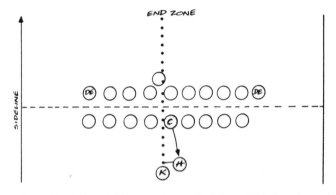

In the Field Goal Formation a field goal kicker has the assistance of a holder, who receives the ball from the snap and places it on the ground in the most convenient position possible for the kicker, who then attempts to place it between the goal posts.

Field Goal Formation

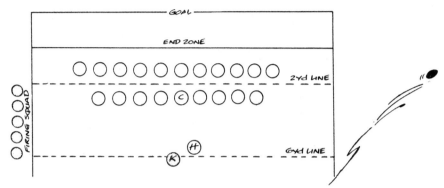

The Touchdown Conversion Formation is almost identical to the Field Goal Formation apart from the special team brought onto the sideline. Placed there for the kicker should he miss the conversion, it's called a firing squad.

CHAPTER 7

SKILLS AND TECHNIQUES

BLOCKING

It is illegal for a blocker to use his hands or feet to stop an opponent, nor may he possess a fire arm or weaponry of any description. A polite verbal request for the opposing player to fall groaning onto the ground will, in most cases, be ignored.

The only course of action left open to him is to drive his shoulders so ferociously into the other player that it bursts several of his internal organs and stops him in his tracks. Ideally he should twist sideways just before the collision and then drop down in the hope of paralysing the player's thighs and putting him out for the rest of the game.

Practising ball skills is of no concern to a blocker, he will probably never have to touch a ball in his playing career. If a ball was ever tossed in his direction he would display the same handling ability as a Sumo wrestler.

A blocker starts practising on inanimate objects, by crashing into sandbags, working up to stunning charging bulls and then by standing in the path of an inter city express train, on the fast section of the track. Finally he can earn his 'Blockers black belt' by facing up to the ultimate challenge, which is done by taking a job as a shop assistant in the ceramics department of Harrods on the first morning of the sale. If he can stay on his feet during the initial rush, after the doors have just been opened, the black belt is his.

TACKLING

Tackling is a technique used to stop the ball-carrying player and to bring him thudding to the ground. The tackler collides with his opponent just above his knees, then lifts and drives him off balance and plasters him onto the pitch. Attempts to separate the tackled player's legs from his body results in more players being injured during tackles than at any other moment in the game apart from the post touchdown celebrations.

Ideally, a large and powerful player should be tackled simultaneously by several defenders to ensure that his progress forwards is restricted. Small players should also be tackled in the same manner to ensure the annual game becomes an anniversary of their demise.

Tripping with a foot is illegal if an official sees it, so is grabbing a player's face mask and swinging him through the air in the hope of tearing off his head. Using a blackjack or any other offensive weapon is also illegal. An extra precaution against illegal play is hoped to be added to the game in the near future. It is called a metal detector and it will scan the players before each match to detect any knuckle dusters concealed on their person. Opponents of this plan claim it will be impractical because so many professional players have had their nasal cartilage rebuilt with steel after continual cocaine abuse destroyed it.

Tackling

HITTING

Hitting will not be found in the coaching manuals. It is an unorthodox though perfectly logical way of stopping a ball-carrying player from driving through the defensive line. Criticism of hitting being too violent doesn't make it any less effective.

A hit is executed by a player who is travelling at maximum speed, who has positioned his helmet in a forwards position while maneouvring his body so that it is parallel to the ground. In this 'torpedo' or 'cruise' position he makes contact with his opponent. It doesn't matter where he makes contact just as long as he makes contact. The ball-carrier will be stopped immediately and whiplashed several yards backwards before being stretchered off the field of combat.

A ball-carrier may adopt the cruise position himself, and so doing will be able to flick a defensive player out of his path like an empty cardboard box. Problems are bound to occur if two players collide when they are both in cruise positions and travelling at maximum speed. The result could possibly be a fracture to the earth's crust, or the entire planet being tilted on its axis and thrown out of orbit onto a collision course with the sun, or at the very worse the ball-carrier may fumble.

Players may practise this technique anywhere there are buildings due for demolition.

Hitting

RUNNING WITH THE BALL (Rushing)

Running while holding a ball is a great deal more difficult than it sounds. Immediately you take hold of the ball (prolate spheroid) you become a target for the hit men (and instantly lose your insurance cover), and it becomes necessary for you to protect the ball with one hand while protecting your life with the other. A coach will tell you that the latter is of no importance and you should use both hands to protect the ball.

If you are an offensive ball carrier it is almost certain a defensive player will shatter your entire being by crashing you to the ground. You will regain consciousness only to discover his hands placed possessively on the ball. He will then say 'Great tackle, man, but get your hands off my ball'. You must not allow your dazed state to confuse you. Never release a ball to an opposing player. If you are in any doubt, wait until officials prise it out of your grasp with crowbars. Secondly, if you regain consciousness to hear 'C'mon man, let go the ball, it's worth a weekend with our most experienced cheerleader in a padlocked attic of your own choice,' your instant response must be to plant your knee into the groin of anyone who also has their hands on the ball. Your team mates will forgive any mistakes, although officials may be less forgiving.

110

Running with the Ball

PASSING

During a game the quarterback does the throwing, apart from the rare occasions when one of the other backs or the end lineman legally throws a pass. Forward passes must be thrown from behind the line of scrimmage. To throw a ball correctly it must be held with the fingers of the throwing hand placed over the laces and with the thumb spread behind the lace. The ball is brought from behind the ear and released with a snap of the wrist so the fingers across the laces cause the ball to spiral through the air.

Do not be deceived by the simplicity of the above description. The heat of the battle, the fading light, the proximity of 300 pound homicidal maniacs lusting after your blood, all combine to make the passer's life more precarious.

A good thrower needs balls for all conditions. He needs balls that drop into receivers' hands from over their shoulders, or fast balls that never stay far off the ground and either remove a layer of skin from the receivers' hands or set them alight. The greater the strength of a passer's balls the better they are for pinpoint accuracy, for throwing into strong winds, and for throwing directly into a linebacker's nuts when death seems the only alternative.

Passing

PUMPING UP

If you're not pumped up don't turn up. Someone who isn't prepared totally to destroy will be totally destroyed. Gridiron is all about commitment, it isn't a game for spineless indifference, wimpoid vacillation or transvestites with wet nail polish. It's kill or be killed.

Every player in the team should be psyched up to a point of spontaneous combustion. This level of manic savagery is attained in the pre-match warm up which includes running through brick walls, treating a bed of nails like a trampoline and by remembering some vile or dirty deed the opposition perpetrated in the last match played against them.

In the dressing room the coach will explain to his players the seriousness of the match. A players parents', his wife's and even his children's and his children's pets' lives depend on the game being won. There will never be a more humiliatingly shameful moment if the game is lost. Not even being stripped naked and hauled behind an incontinent donkey through the streets of the capital.

The last-minute team talk will include asking God for the strength to go out and brutalise the opposition and finishes with a video of Boy George singing 'Do you really want to hurt me . . .'

CHAPTER 8

TECHNICAL TERMS

ANABOLIC STEROID An illegal weight building drug, also known as the 'Footballer's friend'.

ANOREXIC Term used to describe anyone not taking Anabolic Steroids.

AUDIBLE Signals called by the quarterback if he needs to change the play at the line of scrimmage.

"AUDIBLE"

Technical Terms

BACK FIELD The area behind the offensive line.

BLIND SIDE A tackle made usually by a linebacker as he tip-toes up behind the quarterback and tackles him as he throws the ball.

BLITZ A defensive play that sets out to waste the quarterback. The defense commit themselves to the sack but expose themselves at the back, in a cheap attempt to put off the offense.

BOMB A long pass down field, or a quick way of emptying the terraces.

CHAIN GANG Officials who operate a 10 yard chain to accurately measure any dispute for the first down. They are also able to use the chain for self protection against any players who have flipped out on angel dust.

CHUCK An illegal push into another player's back as he waits to receive a pass, or a small gold medallion worn by players who have watched 'Driller Killer' more than one hundred times.

CLIPPING Illegal use of nail cutters to sever laces in an opposing player's pants, officially described as an illegal block from the rear below the waist.

COMPLETION Catching a forward pass, or a successful date.

CUT BACK A side step performed at speed, or a reduced pay packet.

CRACK BACK A cross block where two offensive linemen swap assignments, for example one player going away with another's wife, while the other stays at home with his wife.

CROWD A group of people who attend a football game with the intention of spectating. In the case of a televised game they also attend with the intention of attracting the television cameras, so they can return home and watch themselves on

" THE CROWD "

their video recorders.

The two categories most likely to attract attention consist of blonde females with enormous mammary glands, dressed in tight wet Tee shirts, with printed messages on them, such as 'Go for it!', 'Give the mothers a good kickin'' or 'Hey cameraman fancy a good time in my mobile home, out in the lot?'

The second category consists of complete lunatics wearing absurdly large gloves or unbelievable costumes, and seemingly suffering from severe fits.

Spectators dressed as beer bottles, hamburgers, tins of beans, Snoopy or Yogi Bear are all quite common; an ever decreasing number come as people.

119

Technical Terms

DEAD BALL Once the whistle has blown the ball is no longer live.

DEAD PLAYER Corpse on the pitch, often a quarterback.

DEFENSE The team without the ball, or the lawyers representing the player responsible for the corpse.

DELAY OF GAME The quarterback fails to initiate play within 30 seconds, even though he's physically capable.

DIRECT SNAP When the center snaps the ball back some 5 or 7 yards to a team mate.

DOGGING Another term for blitz, or to eat junk food during the game.

DROP When the quarterback moves into the backfield after the snap to gain more room to manoeuvre, or when a player leaves an amount of money in a prearranged location, to be picked up by a blackmailer who has information concerning him that would be ideal material for the tabloid press.

ENCROACHMENT Illegally zapping an opponent before the snap.

FAKE When a quarterback pretends to do one thing but does another, for example, when he is seen in the company of an attractive cheerleader, when he is really living with the nose tackle.

FLAG ON PLAY When an official's yellow duster appears or when the losing coach waves his white handkerchief.

FLACK JACKET Equipment to protect a player's rib injury or worn by a head coach in sniper country.

FLY PATTERN A defensive formation, when the corner back shouts to a wide receiver, looking up to catch a pass, that his flies are open.

FUMBLE Dropping the ball as a result of an accident or after being tackled, or because of having had a very, very heavy night before.

GOAL LINE The chalk line that separates the field of play from the end zone, not to be mistaken for the chalklines that signify the positions that corpses on the pitch are found in.

HANG TIME The time a punted ball stays in the air.

HAIR OF THE DOG A shot of vodka before the game, or an anti rabies injection.

HAND OFF The transfer of the ball from the quarterback to a running back, or an extremely unpleasant accident.

HASH MARKS Lengthways lines marking the central strip of the field or the burnt parts of the bench where players leave their joints when they are called into the game.

HUDDLE An offensive grouping being told the strategy and code signal for the next play by the quarterback, or when one of the players is showing his team mates compromising photographs of the cheerleader with the mole in the small of her back.

INELIGIBLE RECEIVER A spectator running from the sidelines to catch the ball.

INCOMPLETION An unsuccessful date.

INJURIES Injuries fall into three separate categories. First there are self inflicted injuries that occur when players pump steroids into themselves. Steroids put on muscle and can turn a 230 pound player into a 280 pound player. The rest of the body, alas, is not designed to take on extra weight and he is soon plagued by niggling, almost untraceable tears and pulls. This state of affairs will become worse as larger and larger players are artificially created.

The second category of injuries is caused by artificial surfaces which are universally hated by pro players. The new softer designs are more comfortable to fall on but they also increase traction, leading to knee injuries.

"INJURIES"

The third category consists of injuries inflicted by other players. Naturally, the bigger players get using steroids and the faster they become the worse and more frequent injuries will become. The punishments don't fit the crimes where violent play is concerned. At this evolutionary stage players who splatter other players are, in fact, rewarded in the pro game with more and more money.

Technical Terms

IN MOTION An offensive player, not on the line, running laterally before the snap.

INTENTIONAL GROUNDING A quarterback deliberately throwing the ball away while pretending that it's an accident and then being told by an official that as a punishment he can't go out at night, for a month.

KNUCKLE BALL A term from baseball describing how instead of the ball rotating on its axis through the air, it tumbles.

KNUCKLE SANDWICH A blow with a clenched fist delivered through the defensive face guard of the victim, with the intention of rotating him on his axis, or ass.

KHYBER PASS A strategic gap in a mountain range on the Indian subcontinent.

LATERAL PASS A rugby-style pass backwards or sideways.

LINE DRIVE A ball kicked very hard and far which travels almost parallel to the ground.

LINE MAN A player hit very hard and far who travels almost parallel to the ground.

MOAN A noise made by a player after receiving a knuckle sandwich.

MUFF Where a player touches a free ball but is unsuccessful in gaining possession of it, or to carry a post touchdown embrace too far.

NEUTRAL ZONE The 11 inch strip of ground (a football's length) straddling the line of scrimmage.

NEUTERED The condition of a player involved in an unfortunate accident while straddling the line of scrimmage.

OFFENSIVE HOLDING A player grabbing hold of another player in a way that off the field would get him two years in a moral correction centre.

123

Technical Terms

OFFICIALS There are seven different officials in a football game. The main man is the referee, then we have the umpire, the head linesman, followed by the line judge, the back judge, the side judge and the field judge.

The referee is the official who stands in the middle of the field while he waves his hands and arms about. The arm waving is not a nervous reaction to stress, it has a meaning behind it. The following illustrations explain some of these gestures.

IT'S TOO LATE FOR A DOCTOR JUST BRING ON A BODY BAG

THERE ARE TOO MANY COKE DEALERS ON THE SIDELINES

I'LL HAVE A HOT DOG AT HALF TIME THIS BIG

GET THE ARMOURED TRUCK RUNNING, I'M ABOUT TO MAKE ANOTHER BUM DECISION

OFFSIDE A lineman who is beyond the line of scrimmage when the ball is snapped.
ONSIDE A short kick by the offense in a desperate attempt to keep possession of the ball.

"PASS INTERFERENCE"

PASS INTERFERENCE A landslide in the Khyber, or grabbing, gouging or goosing in an illegal attempt to catch or intercept a forward pass.

PENALTY MARKER See Flag on play.

PERSONAL FOUL An act of violent contact, kicking, punching or using a meat hook on the field of play.

PILING ON The illegal act of deliberately leaping onto an opponent's haemorrhoids.

PLAY ACTION The movement of a quarterback just before delivering a pass. He may be moving from one side to another or hiding in the pocket.

"STUNTING"

Technical Terms

POCKET The area protected by the offensive line where the quarterback hides.

ROUGHING THE KICKER Illegal violent acts on the kicker after he has kicked the ball.

RUSHING PLAY Running with the ball after the handoff.

SACK Tackling the quarterback while he still holds the ball.

SHIFT The movement of offensive players immediately prior to the snap.

SNAP The most common sound accompanying a hit.

SPIKING The flamboyant act of throwing the ball as hard as possible into the ground by the player who has scored a touchdown.

SPEARING The flamboyant act of a player diving headfirst onto a player who has just scored a touchdown.

STUNTING When an outside linebacker loops around an inside linebacker to pierce the middle of the offensive line, or when a quarterback is lifted by a larger defensive player and hammered headfirst into the ground in an attempt to reduce his height.

TELEVISION A football fan unable to watch a game in the flesh has to watch it on television. To do this correctly he needs an armchair, a minimum of two six packs of beer and a megaphone. The armchair is to support him in a sitting position, the beer is to make sure he keeps his circulation going by having to get up every ten minutes to take a leak, and the megaphone is to ensure the whole neighbourhood knows when the game either pleases or displeases him.

TIME OUT The game clock is stopped running at the request of the captains or the officials.

TWO MINUTE WARNING An automatic time out occurring two minutes before the end of each half, or when unidentified missiles appear on radar coming over the polar cap.

THE END